Trader Joe's Cookbook made simple: Healthy, Easy, Quick meals in 15 minutes or less.

First Edition

Your feedback is greatly appreciated!

It's through your feedback, support and reviews that I'm able to create the best books possible and serve more people. I would be extremely grateful if you could take just 60 seconds to kindly leave an honest review of the book on Amazon. Please share your feedback and thoughts for others to see. To do so, simply find the book on Amazon's website (or wherever you purchased the book from) and locate the section to leave a review. Select a star rating and write a couple of sentences.

That's it! Thank you so much for your support.

Review this product

Share your thoughts with other customers

Table of Content

BREAKFAST

1. Apple Cinnamon Breakfast Quinoa

Ingredients:

- ½ cup Trader Joe's Organic Quinoa
- 1 cup water or almond milk
- ½ apple, diced
- 1 tablespoon chopped walnuts
- ½ teaspoon cinnamon
- 1 tablespoon maple syrup

Directions

1. Rinse quinoa under cold water. In a small saucepan, combine quinoa and water or almond milk.

2. Bring to a boil, then reduce heat and simmer for 15 minutes or until quinoa is cooked and liquid is absorbed.

3.. Stir in diced apple, chopped walnuts, cinnamon, and maple syrup. Serve warm.

Nutritional Fact

Serving:	0.5cup
Calories:	155kcal
Carbohydrates:	29g
Protein:	4g
Fat:	3g

Saturated Fat:	1g
Sodium:	84mg
Potassium:	230mg
Fiber:	5g
Sugar:	11g
Vitamin A:	37IU
Vitamin C:	3mg
Calcium:	111mg
Iron:	1mg

2. Spinach and Feta Omelette

Ingredients:

- 2 eggs
- Handful of fresh spinach
- ¼ cup crumbled feta cheese
- 1 tablespoon olive oil
- Salt and pepper to taste
- 2 or three big eggs;
- 1 tablespoon unsalted butter;
- 1/4 cup crumbled feta (or goat cheese);
- 2 tablespoons chopped fresh chives (optional) for garnish

Directions

1. In a bowl, whisk together eggs, salt, and pepper. Heat olive oil in a skillet over medium heat.

2. Pour the egg mixture into the skillet and swirl to coat the bottom.

3. Cook until the edges start to set.

4. Add spinach and feta cheese to one half of the omelette.

5. Fold the other half over the filling and cook until the cheese is melted and the omelette is cooked through.

Nutritional Fact

Calories:	368KCAL
Carbohydrates:	3G
Protein:	17G
Fat:	32G
Saturated Fat:	16G
Polyunsaturated Fat:	3G
Monounsaturated Fat:	11G
Trans Fat:	1G
Cholesterol:	391MG
Sodium:	569MG
Potassium:	321MG
Fiber:	1G
Sugar:	2G
Vitamin A:	3883IU
Vitamin C:	10MG
Calcium:	269MG
Iron:	3MG

3. Avocado Toast with Poached Egg

Ingredients:

- 2 slices Trader Joe's whole grain bread
- 1 ripe avocado
- 2 eggs
- Salt and pepper to taste
- 1/3 avocado (I don't always use it all; I usually cut it in half). Alright, I guess I might.)
- Quartered heirloom tomatoes should be topped with two tablespoons of shaved Parmesan cheese, salt, and pepper, and fresh herbs like basil, thyme, or parsley.

Directions

1. Toast the whole grain bread slices.

2. Mash the ripe avocado and spread it evenly on the toasted bread.

3. Poach the eggs and place one on each slice of avocado toast.

4. Season with salt and pepper to taste.

5. Toast the bread and mash the avocado into each slice of toast while the eggs cook.

6. Once cooked, remove the eggs from the water using a spatula.

7. Remove the egg rims gently (I do this right over the water with the spatula) and arrange the poached eggs on top of the toast.

8. Season with salt, pepper, Parmesan cheese, and fresh herbs. Present alongside freshly quartered heirloom tomatoes.

Nutritional Fact

Total Fat	20.4g
Cholesterol	334.6mg
Sodium	499.7mg
Total Carbohydrate	30.1g
Dietary Fiber	7.7g
Sugars	5.7g
Protein	23.3g
Vitamin A	195.4µg
Vitamin C	13.4mg
Iron	3.4mg
Potassium	641.5mg
Phosphorus	407.1mg

4. Overnight Oats with Peanut Butter and Banana

Ingredients:

- ½ cup Trader Joe's Rolled Oats
- ½ cup almond milk
- 1 tablespoon peanut butter
- ½ banana, sliced
- 1 tablespoon honey

Directions

1. In a jar or bowl, mix rolled oats and almond milk.

2. Stir in peanut butter and honey. Top with sliced banana.

3. Cover and refrigerate overnight.

4. Enjoy the cold in the morning.

Nutritional Fact

Serving Size:	1/3 of recipe
Calories:	290
Fat:	10 g
Sodium:	65 mg
Carbohydrate:	40 g

Fiber:	7 g
Sugar:	12 g
Protein:	12g

5. Spinach and Tomato Breakfast Quesadilla

Ingredients:

- 1 Trader Joe's Whole Wheat Tortilla
- Handful of fresh spinach
- 2 slices tomato
- ¼ cup shredded mozzarella cheese
- 1 egg, scrambled (optional)

Directions

1. Heat a skillet over medium heat. Place the whole wheat tortilla in the skillet. Layer fresh spinach, tomato slices, shredded mozzarella cheese, and scrambled egg (if using) on one half of the tortilla.

2. Fold the other half over the filling and cook until the tortilla is golden and the cheese is melted.

3. Flip and cook until the other side is golden. Cut into wedges and serve.

Nutritional Fact

Serving:	1Quesadilla
Calories:	340kcal
Carbohydrates:	23g
Protein:	30g
Saturated Fat:	5g
Cholesterol:	401mg

Sodium:	823mg
Fiber:	3g
Sugar:	3g

6. Banana Nut Oatmeal

Ingredients:

- 1 cup Trader Joe's Rolled Oats
- 1 ripe banana, mashed
- 2 tablespoons chopped walnuts
- 1 tablespoon honey
- Pinch of cinnamon
- ½ tsp ground cinnamon, optional
- ½ tsp vanilla essence, optional **banana** cut, toasted,
- 2 Tablespoons walnuts,
- 1 Tablespoon peanut butter, and 1/2 tsp chia seeds

Directions

1. Cook rolled oats according to package instructions.

2. Stir in mashed banana, chopped walnuts, honey, and a pinch of cinnamon.

3. Place the oats in a bowl and garnish with toasted walnuts, peanut butter, banana slices, and chia seeds.

4. While the food is cooking, you can also add the banana slices.

5. The oats will get a lot of flavor and sweetness from the banana.

6. Serve hot.

Nutritional Fact

Serving:	1bowl made with water (no toppings)
Calories:	153kcal
Carbohydrates:	27g
Protein:	5g
Fat:	3g
Saturated Fat:	1g
Sodium:	157mg
Fiber:	4g
Sugar:	1g

7. Breakfast Burrito

Ingredient

- Peel and grate two big russet potatoes.
- 1 pound breakfast sausage in the ground
- 6 big, beaten eggs
- 1 tsp sea salt and ¼ tsp freshly ground black pepper
- 2 tsp extra virgin olive oil
- 6 10-inch flour tortillas and four chopped green onions
- 2 cups of cheddar cheese, grated
- 2 avocados, cut and pitted
- 1/4 cup salsa
- ¼ cup finely chopped, raw cilantro leaves

Direction

1. Squeeze as much moisture out of the potatoes as you can by placing them in a cheesecloth or fresh kitchen towel.
2. Over medium heat, preheat a large nonstick skillet.
3. As soon as the skillet is heated, add the sausage and cook it for about five minutes, breaking up the meat with a wooden spoon, until it is browned and cooked through. Shift over to a platter.

Nutritional Fact

Calories534

Protein31 g

Carbohydrates29 g

Total Fat36 g

Dietary Fiber6 g

Cholesterol268 mg

sodium1178 mg

Total Sugars3 g

8. Berry Smoothie

Ingredient

- 3 cups of mixed berries, frozen
- 1 sliced frozen banana
- ½ a cup of plain yogurt for
- ½ a teaspoon vanilla extract
- 1 tablespoon of sugar
- 1 ½ cups of almond milk, unsweetened
- 1 ½ cups apple juice
- 1 sliced banana, or any other juice flavor
- ¾ cup vanilla Greek yogurt;
- 1 ½ cups frozen mixed berries; optional
- 1 tablespoon honeyFresh berries and mint sprigs are an optional garnish.

Direction

1. In a big blender, add the frozen mixed berries, yogurt, sugar, vanilla essence, frozen banana cut in half, and almond milk.
2. Pure the mixture until it's smooth.
3. Add extra milk as necessary to thin the smoothie to the desired consistency.
4. Enjoy it soon after serving.

Nutritional Fact

Calories: 261kcal

Carbohydrates: 52g

Protein: 5gFat: 6g

Sodium: 275mg

Fiber: 8g

9. Protein Pancakes

Ingredient

- Just one banana
- 75g of oats
- 3 huge eggs
- 2 tablespoons milk (you can use nut, soy, dairy, or oat milks)
- 1-tablespoon baking powder
- A small amount of cinnamon
- 2 tablespoons of protein powder
- Coconut oil or a flavorless oil to cook berries
- Sliced banana, maple syrup, and nut butter to serve

Direction

1. In a blender, combine the banana, oats, eggs, milk, baking powder, cinnamon, and protein powder for one to two minutes, or until smooth.
2. If the oats haven't broken down, give them another minute to combine.
3. In a pan, warm up a drizzle of oil.
4. Ladle or pour in two to three rounds of batter, allowing some room for the batter to spread in between.
5. Simmer for a minute or two, or until the underside turns golden and bubbles begin to form on the top.
6. After a minute, turn over and continue cooking until done.
7. After transferring to a preheated oven, repeat with the leftover batter.
8. Arrange fruit, maple syrup, and nut butter in stacks and serve.

Nutritional Fact

Kcal437

Fat16g

Saturates4g

Carbs39g

Sugars9g

Fibre4g

Protein 31g

salt1.4g

10. Chia Pudding

Ingredient

- One scoop (25 grams) of vanilla protein powder;
- 1.5 to 2 cups of unsweetened vanilla almond milk, or more as necessary;
- 4 Tablespoons of chia seeds;
- ½ Tablespoon of maple syrup, honey, or other preferred sweetener;
- ¼ teaspoon of optional vanilla extract;
- ½ cup of Greek yogurt (or non-dairy yogurt);
- Granola, to garnishGranola, nut butter, and fresh berries are the toppings.

Direction

1. Protein powder and almond milk should be combined in a dish or mason jar and whisked until the powder dissolves.
2. If you're using a mason jar, you can mix the mixture by shaking it after covering it.
3. Add vanilla, maple syrup, and chia seeds.
4. When ready to serve, divide the chia pudding into two glasses and top with granola, if preferred.
5. Add your preferred toppings, such as more granola, nut butter, fresh berries, or ¼ cup Greek yogurt for each person.

Nutritional Fact

Serving: 1/2 without toppings |

Calories: 243kcal |

Carbohydrates: 13g |

Protein: 19g |

Fat: 14g |

Saturated Fat: 3g |

Polyunsaturated Fat: 6g |

Monounsaturated Fat: 2g |

Sodium: 299mg |

Potassium: 288mg |

Fiber: 6g |

Sugar: 3g

11. Smoked Salmon Bagel

Ingredient

- 1 tablespoon fresh dill plus extra for serving,
- ½ bagels,
- 4 ounces thinly sliced smoked salmon,
- 4 ounces cream cheese,
- 2 tablespoons lemon juice
- 1 or 2 Persian cucumbers, peeled and cut into ribbons.
- Salt and pepper to taste.
- Slicing red onions for serving
- Taste-tested capers

Direction

1. Mix the cream cheese, fresh dill, lemon juice, and salt and pepper to taste in a small bowl.
2. Spread the cream cheese mixture over the top and bottom of the toasted bagels.
3. Toasted bagels should include cucumbers, smoked salmon, capers, and red onions on the bottom.

Nutritional Fact

Serving: 1bagel

Calories: 395kcal

Carbohydrates: 45g

Protein: 23gFat: 10g

Sodium: 891mg

Potassium: 258mg

Fiber: 3g

Vitamin A: 390IU

Vitamin C: 3mg

Calcium: 109mg

Iron: 3mg

NET CARBS: 42g

12.Peanut Butter and Jelly Oats

Ingredient

- 1/2 cup of rolled oats free of gluten
- Equina flakes, half a cup
- 2 cups water
- 1/4 cup of creamy peanut butter
- 2 teaspoons of maple syrup plus extra for the garnish
- a dash of cinnamon
- 1 teaspoon of vanilla essence or one pinch of powdered vanilla
- I used this recipe (but only with raspberries) to make 1/4 cup of divided chia seed jam.
- Shredded coconut is not required.

Direction

1. Fill a small saucepan with oats, water, and quinoa flakes.
2. After bringing to a boil, lower the heat to a simmer and cook for two to three minutes, stirring often.
3. Stir in the peanut butter, syrup, and spices when the oats have begun to soften but the mixture is still runny, and simmer until it becomes thick and creamy.

Nutritional Fact

Calories: 455kcal

Carbohydrates: 65g

Protein: 13g

Fat: 19g

Saturated Fat: 3g

Sodium: 165mg

Potassium: 346mg

Fiber: 6g

Sugar: 27g

Calcium: 54mg

Iron: 2.7mg

13. Coconut Yogurt Bowl

Ingredient

- One cup (245g) of coconut yogurt;
- thirty grams of raspberries;
- thirty grams of blueberries;
- sixty grams of oats
- One sliced tiny banana, if desired
- One tablespoon (12g) of chia seeds
- one tablespoon (20g) of maple syrup, agave nectar, coconut nectar, etc. (optional)

Direction

1. Put the yogurt made of coconut in a medium-sized bowl.
2. Add fruit to the yogurt, such as bananas, chia seeds, oats, and berries.
3. Sweetener (if using) can be drizzled on.
4. In accordance, serve.

Nutritional Fact

Calories: 376kcal |

Carbohydrates: 63g |

Protein: 11g | Fat: 9g |

Saturated Fat: 14g |

Polyunsaturated Fat: 3g |

Monounsaturated Fat: 1g |

Trans Fat: 0.02g |

Sodium: 35mg |

Potassium: 241mg |

Fiber: 10g |

Sugar: 25g |

Vitamin A: 36IU |

Vitamin C: 42mg |

Calcium: 417mg |

Iron: 2mg

14. Ricotta and Berry Toast

Ingredient

- 2 pieces of artisan bread or your preferred bread
- To fry bread, use two tablespoons of butter.
- 1/2 cup of ricotta
- 1 tablespoon of honey
- 1/2 teaspoon of cinnamon
- 1 cup of sliced strawberries and a 6-ounce bag of raspberries
- Add a tablespoon of sugar and garnish with optional basil, mint leaves, lemon or orange zest.

Direction

1. Strawberries are best cleaned, cut, and then put in a small bowl.
2. Clean, then add raspberries. After dusting with sugar, place aside.
3. Cut the bread into slices and place two tablespoons of butter in a big skillet.
4. Take the bread out of the heat source and fry it until it becomes crispy on both sides.
5. Blend or process the ricotta cheese, honey, and cinnamon in a food processor.
6. Mix for one to two minutes, or until smooth and light.
7. Mash the berries with a fork, following the directions in the post.

15. Cottage Cheese and Fruit Bowl

Ingredient

- A cup of fresh mixed berries, peaches, cherries, mangoes, kiwis, or peaches;
- 8 ounces of cottage cheese;
- 1-2 teaspoons of honey;Optional: Flaxseed, granola, and chia seeds
- 2 cups cottage cheese
- 1 cup of raw berries
- 1/4 cup granola,
- 1/4 tablespoon honey

Direction

1. In a food processor or small blender, combine cottage cheese and honey.
2. Using a rubber spatula to scrape down the sides as necessary to combine evenly, blend until smooth and fluffy.
3. Place the whipped cottage cheese in a bowl, then garnish with the desired amount of fruit and other toppings.
4. Chill and serve.

Nutritional Fact

Calories: 301kcal

Carbohydrates: 27g

Protein: 26g

Fat: 11g

Saturated Fat: 4g

Polyunsaturated Fat: 1g

Monounsaturated Fat: 2g

Cholesterol: 39mg

Sodium: 302mg

Potassium: 320mg

Fiber: 4g

Sugar: 12g

Vitamin A: 389IU

Vitamin C: 4mg

Calcium: 201mg

Iron: 0.4mg

16. Veggie and Egg Scramble

Ingredient

- 2 tsp extra virgin olive oil or any other type of cooking oil
- 4 big eggs, lightly beaten; one cup chopped mixed vegetables, such as peppers, mushrooms, onions, and zucchini
- 1/8 teaspoon salt, or to taste
- freshly ground pepper according to flavor
- A pinch of salt-free spice, like Mrs. Dash
- 3 tsp of Parmesan cheese

Direction

1. Fill a big nonstick skillet with oil and heat it over medium-high heat.
2. When the vegetables are tender and browned in places, add them and simmer, stirring frequently, for 2 to 4 minutes.
3. Meanwhile, in a small mixing bowl, whisk together eggs, salt, pepper, and seasoning without salt.

Nutritional Fact

Serving Size: *1 cup*

Calories: *243*

Sugar: *0 g*

Fat: *16 g*

Saturated Fat: *5 g*

Carbohydrates: *7 g*

Protein: *16 g*

17. Oatmeal with Fresh Fruit

Ingredient

- 3 cups of rolled oats, sometimes referred to as "old-fashioned oatmeal";
- 2 teaspoons of cinnamon;
- 1 teaspoon of optional pure vanilla extract; milk for serving; and sliced nuts, hemp seeds, chia seeds, and nut butter (optional for serving)
- 3 cups of strawberries, peaches, mango, blueberries, or frozen blueberries
- 1 cup mashed banana, applesauce, raisins, dried cherries, chopped dry apples, or dried cranberries
- 1 cup shredded apple

Direction

1. In a medium pot, bring 4 cups of water to a boil over high heat.
2. Add the oats, cinnamon, and vanilla when the mixture is almost boiling, then lower the heat to medium.
3. Stir frequently and cook for about 4 minutes, or until the oats are mushy and the water is absorbed.
4. Stir in your preferred fruit.

Nutritional Fact

Calories: 199kcal,

Carbohydrates: 39g,

Protein: 6g, Fat: 3g,

Saturated Fat: 1g,

Polyunsaturated Fat: 1g,

Monounsaturated Fat: 1g,

Sodium: 3mg,

Potassium: 207mg,

Fiber: 6g, Sugar: 8g,

Vitamin A: 42IU,

Vitamin C: 7mg,

Calcium: 32mg,

Iron: 2mg

18. Breakfast Flatbread

Ingredient

- 1 big flatbread
- 2 tablespoons of olive oil, split
- 1 cup of shredded cheddar cheese
- 4 chunks of squared-up Canadian bacon
- Diced ¼ cup of red peppers
- cut three to four asparagus spears
- 2 huge eggs
- 1/3 tsp everything bagel spice
- Shredded Parmesan cheese, two tablespoons
- 1 tablespoon finely chopped parsley

Direction

1. Turn the oven on to 450 degrees.
2. The Canadian bacon should be pan-fried for one to two minutes on each side in a big pan with one tablespoon of olive oil over medium heat before being removed.
3. Remove the chopped asparagus spears and red pepper and onion from the pan after they have sautéed for two to three minutes.
4. Bake the flatbread for 8 to 10 minutes, or until it's golden brown and the egg whites are just starting to set.

5. Take out of the oven, sprinkle with the parsley, and serve right away.

Nutritional Fact

Calories: 547

Total Fat: 24g

Saturated Fat: 9g

Trans Fat: 0g

Unsaturated Fat: 14g

Cholesterol: 406mg

Sodium: 1021mg

Carbohydrates: 51g

Fiber: 3g

Sugar: 3g

Protein: 29g

19. Muesli and Yogurt Bowl

Ingredient

- 1/4 cup muesli
- 1/2 cup of coconut yogurt
- 1/4 cup blueberries
- 1/4 cup blackberries
- 1/4 cup of papaya, chopped
- 1 spoonful of chia seeds
- 1/4 cup almond milk

Direction

1. Fill a bowl with your Greek yogurt.
2. Any variety of Greek yogurt will work just fine!
3. Just watch out that there isn't an excessive amount of added sugar.
4. The mixed berries should then be added to the Greek yogurt.
5. Use the microwave to defrost any frozen berries you plan to use.
6. Alternatively, you might leave them out overnight in the refrigerator to thaw naturally.
7. Top with your muesli and savor!

Nutritional Fact

Calories: 345kcal

Carbohydrates: 55g

Protein: 17g

Fat: 5g

Fiber: 8g

Vitamin C: 18mg

Calcium: 84mg

20. Nut Butter and Berry Toast

Ingredient

- 1 whole grain English muffin
- 2 tablespoons of almond butter or your preferred nut butter
- 1/2 cup of your preferred fresh berry toppings
- 1 tablespoon of chia or crushed flax seeds to drizzle over honey

Direction

1. Arrange the fresh berries on top of the toast after spreading it with almond butter.
2. After serving, top with hemp or chia/coconut flakes.
3. Halve the English muffin if necessary.
4. Toast to the right level of doneness.
5. Arrange nut butter on top of an English muffin.
6. After adding the chosen toppings, savor!

Nutritional Fact

Calories	63 Kcal
Protein	1g
Carbs	3g
Fat	5g
Fiber	1g
Sugar	1g

21.Pumpkin Spice Oatmeal

Ingredient

- 1 and a half cups water and 1/4 cup maple syrup
- 1/3 cup pureed pumpkin
- 1 cup of quick oats
- 1/8 teaspoon salt
- 1/4 Pumpkin Pie Spice
- 1 cup of skim milk
- Pumpkin pie spice, 1/4 tsp
- Sugar, half a tablespoon
- 1/2 tsp vanilla extract and 1/16 tsp of salt

Direction

1. On the stovetop, place a pot. Stir with water and maple syrup. Stir to incorporate.
2. Stir in quick oats and pumpkin puree next. Mix well to blend.
3. Add pumpkin pie spice and salt. Mix all items in pot with a stir.
4. After setting the cooktop to medium-high, cook for about five minutes. stirring every now and then.
5. Turn off the burner and dish the thickened oatmeal into separate serving bowls.

22. Tropical Smoothie Bowl

Ingredient

- 1 tiny ripe mango that has been stoned, skinned, and sliced into bits
- 200g of cored, peeled, and chunked pineapple
- 2 bananas that are ripe
- 2 tablespoons of coconut yogurt—not yogurt with coconut flavor—
- 150ml of drinking milk made from coconuts
- ½ passion fruits, remove the seeds, and take a handful of blueberries.
- 2 tsp of coconut flakes
- a couple leaves of mint

Direction

1. In a blender, combine the mango, pineapple, bananas, yogurt, and coconut milk; process until smooth and thick.
2. Transfer the mixture between two bowls and garnish with the blueberries, passion fruit, coconut flakes, and mint leaves.
3. Will last for one day when refrigerated.
4. Serve immediately after adding the toppings.

Nutritional Fact

Calories: 180kcal,

Carbohydrates: 44g,

Protein: 3g, Fat: 1g,

Saturated Fat: 0.1g,

Polyunsaturated Fat: 0.4g,

Monounsaturated Fat: 0.2g,

Sodium: 6mg,

Potassium: 706mg,

Fiber: 9g,

Sugar: 34g,

Vitamin A: 1213IU,

Vitamin C: 227mg,

Calcium: 98mg,

Iron: 1mg

LUNCH

23. Veggie and Hummus Wrap

Ingredients:

- 1 Trader Joe's Whole Wheat Tortilla
- 2 tablespoons Trader Joe's Hummus
- ¼ cup shredded carrots
- ¼ cup sliced cucumber
- ¼ cup sliced bell peppers
- Handful of mixed greens

Directions

1. Spread hummus evenly over the whole wheat tortilla.

2. Layer shredded carrots, sliced cucumber, sliced bell peppers, and mixed greens on top.

3. Roll up the tortilla tightly, slice in half, and serve.

Nutritional Fact

Calories:	285kcal
Carbohydrates:	39g
Protein:	7g
Fat:	12g
Saturated Fat:	2g
Polyunsaturated Fat:	2g
Monounsaturated Fat:	7g

Trans Fat:	74g
Sodium:	517mg
Potassium:	385mg
Fiber:	3g
Sugar:	6g
Vitamin A:	3473IU
Vitamin C:	62mg
Calcium:	95mg
Iron:	3mg

24. Tuna Salad Lettuce Wraps

Ingredients:

- 1 can Trader Joe's Albacore Tuna in Olive Oil, drained
- 2 tablespoons mayonnaise
- 1 tablespoon chopped celery
- 1 tablespoon chopped red onion
- 1 teaspoon Dijon mustard
- Salt and pepper to taste
- Butter lettuce leaves

Directions

1. In a bowl, mix together tuna, mayonnaise, chopped celery, chopped red onion, Dijon mustard, salt, and pepper.

2. Spoon the tuna salad onto butter lettuce leaves.

3. Remove 8 large leaves from the lettuce head by chopping it apart. (I preserved the smaller inner leaves of the two heads of romaine for salad greens.)

4. When drying lettuce, use paper towels or a salad spinner if necessary.

5. Using your hands, assemble the tuna mixture into two heaping tablespoons per lettuce leaf, top with a mixture of cherry tomatoes and avocados, and serve.

6. Roll up and serve.

Nutritional Fact

Calories:	314
Total Fat:	24g
Saturated Fat:	3.8g
Trans Fat:	0g
Unsaturated Fat:	18.3g
Cholesterol:	36mg
Sodium:	559mg
Carbohydrates:	8.5g
Fiber:	5g
Sugar:	2.2g
Protein:	19g

25. Greek Yogurt Chicken Salad

Ingredients:

- 2 cups cooked shredded chicken
- 1/2 cup Greek yogurt
- 1/4 cup diced celery
- 1/4 cup diced red onion
- 1/4 cup halved grapes
- 1/4 cup chopped walnuts
- 2 tablespoons chopped fresh dill
- Juice of 1 lemon
- Salt and black pepper, to taste

Directions:

1. In a bowl, combine shredded chicken,

2. Greek yogurt, diced celery, diced red onion, halved grapes, chopped walnuts, chopped dill, and lemon juice.

3. Season with salt and black pepper. Mix well. Serve chilled on sandwiches, wraps, or salads.

Nutritional fact

SERVING: 1(of 6), about 1 cup

CALORIES: 228kcal

CARBOHYDRATES: 17g

PROTEIN: 27gFAT: 6g

CHOLESTEROL: 48mg

SODIUM: 327mg

FIBER: 2g

SUGAR: 12g

26. Mediterranean Hummus Platter

Ingredient

- 2 cups Tzatziki sauce
- 2 cups hummus
- 1 jar sun-dried tomato pesto
- 2 cups marinated feta cheese
- 2 cups marinated olives
- Persian cucumbers
- cherry tomatoes
- avocado chunks combined with lemon juice and sea salt; assorted fruits, cherries, peaches, berries, and figs
- 1 bunch of delicious flowers or fresh herbs

Directions

1. Ensure that every component is nearly at room temperature.

2. Place every component on a sizable dish or chopping board. Over the hummus and Tzatziki, drizzle some vinaigrette or olive oil. Arrange the crackers, pita chips, and various pita on the platter. As desired, garnish with edible flowers and herbs.

27. Greek Orzo Salad

Ingredients:

- 1 cup cooked Trader Joe's Organic Orzo Pasta
- 1/2 cup diced cucumbers
- 1/2 cup halved cherry tomatoes
- 1/4 cup diced red onion
- 1/4 cup crumbled feta cheese
- 2 tablespoons chopped fresh parsley
- 2 tablespoons lemon juice
- 1 tablespoon olive oil
- Salt and black pepper, to taste

Directions:

1. In a medium mixing bowl whisk together olive oil, lemon juice, garlic and season with salt and pepper to taste, set aside.
2. Cook orzo according to directions listed on the package to al dente or just 1 minute shy. Drain and rinse under cold water for about 10 seconds. Drain well.
3. Add all of the salad ingredients, including cooked orzo, to a large bowl and toss. Pour dressing over top and toss to evenly coat.
4. Store in the refrigerator for up to 2 days.

Nutrition facts:

- Amount Per Serving
- Fat 19g29%
- Saturated Fat 5g31%
- Cholesterol 22mg7%
- Sodium 458mg20%
- Potassium 199mg6%
- Carbohydrates 28g9%
- Fiber 1g4%
- Sugar 3g3%
- Protein 8g16%
- Vitamin A 400IU8%
- Vitamin C 7.8mg9%
- Calcium 151mg15%
- Iron 1mg6%
- * Percent Daily Values are based on a 2000 calorie diet.
- Nutrition values are estima

28. Southwest Quinoa Salad

Ingredients:

- 1 cup of quinoa
- 2 cups water
- A kosher pinch of salt
- 15-ounce can of rinsed and drained black beans
- 1 chopped red bell pepper
- 1 cup of chopped grape tomatoes
- 1 cup fresh corn, uncooked or burnt
- 1/2 cup diced red onion and one big avocado, chopped
- Add black pepper and kosher salt to taste.
- Lime and Cilantro Salad

Directions:

1. Put the quinoa through a sieve and rinse it with cool water.
2. Fill a medium saucepan with quinoa, water, and salt; cook over medium heat until boiling.
3. For five minutes, boil. Simmer until the water is absorbed, turning down the heat to low for about 15 minutes.
4. Take off the heat source and mix with a fork.
5. After quinoa cools to room temperature, stir it.
6. Mix thoroughly after adding a drizzle of cilantro-lime vinaigrette. If required, add more salt and pepper after tasting. Assemble!

Nutrition facts:

Calories: 194kcal,

Carbohydrates: 31g,

Protein: 8g,

Fat: 5g,

Saturated Fat: 1g,

Polyunsaturated Fat: 1g,

Monounsaturated Fat: 3g,

Trans Fat: 0.001g,

Sodium: 215mg,

Potassium: 544mg,

Fiber: 8g,

Sugar: 3g,

Vitamin A: 697IU,

Vitamin C: 28mg,

Calcium: 39mg,

Iron: 2mg

29. Crunchy Asian Slaw

Ingredients

- 3 cups of Chinese cabbage, chopped or shredded;
- 3 cups of red cabbage;
- 2 large carrots, chopped or julienned;
- 3 cups of bean sprouts;
- 3 green onions, chopped finely on the diagonal
- Thumbnails of rice vinegar
- 2 tsp fish sauce, or extra soy
- 2 tbsp lime juice, or extra rice vinegar

Directions:

1. Put all of the dressing ingredients in a jar and give it a good shake.
2. Mix all of the salad ingredients together, excluding the Asian Fried Shallots.
3. Drizzle with dressing and toss to mix.
4. Shred the cabbage finely till you get 3–4 cups of it. Cut the apple into thin matchsticks after slicing it thinly. After peeling, chop the carrot into thin matchsticks, shred it, or finely grate it.

30Caesar Salad with Kale

Ingredients

- 1 bunch of stemmed curly kale
- 1 tsp pure virgin olive oil
- sea salt
- 5 cups of romaine lettuce, chopped
- Make Your Own or Use a Vegan Caesar Dressing
- 1-cup Croutons Made at Home
- vegan or shaved Parmesan cheese Cheese Parmesan
- optional roasted chickpeas
- 1 diced avocado, if desired

Directions:

1. Chop the kale into small pieces and transfer it to a big basin.
2. Add a drizzle of olive oil and a small teaspoon of salt.
3. Till the leaves wilt, massage them with your hands.
4. Throw in the romaine and mix.
5. After adding half of the dressing, toss once more.
6. Spoon into a serving bowl, then sprinkle the Parmesan and croutons on top.
7. If preferred, top with avocado, roasted chickpeas, and more dressing before serving.

Nutrition facts:

Kcal 378

Fat 25g

Saturate 4g

Carbs 21g

Sugars 4g

Fibre 7g

Protein 13g

Salt 1.1g

31. Spicy Buffalo Chicken Wrap

Ingredients

- 4 large flour tortillas;
- 1/2 cup blue cheese or ranch dressing;
- 2 cups chopped Romaine lettuces;
- 1/2 cup shredded carrot;
- 1 pound boneless, skinless chicken breasts;
- 2 Tablespoons olive oil;
- 1/2 cup Frank's Hot Sauce;
- 1/2 teaspoon paprika;
- 1/2 teaspoon garlic powder; pinch of salt;
- 1/2 sliced avocado
- 1/2 cup of shredded cheddar cheese

Directions:

1. Cut the chicken breast into a number of long, narrow strips.
2. Combine salt, garlic powder, paprika, spicy sauce, and olive oil in a small bowl.
3. Add the chicken and marinate it for ten minutes or longer, up to twenty-four hours.
4. Place the chicken strips in a sizable nonstick skillet and heat it to medium-high.

Nutrition facts:

Calories: 526kcal

Carbohydrates: 22g

Protein: 31g

Fat: 34g

Saturated Fat: 8g

Polyunsaturated Fat: 10g

Monounsaturated Fat: 13g

Trans Fat: 0.01g

Cholesterol: 95mg

Sodium: 1523mg

Potassium: 772mg

Fiber: 4g

Sugar: 4g

Vitamin A: 5115IU

Vitamin C: 28mg

Calcium: 177mg

Iron: 2mg

32. California turkey avocado Sandwich

Ingredients

- 8pieces of bread
- 4 lettuce leaves
- 1 pound of sliced turkey
- 8 slices of tomato
- Add salt and pepper to taste.
- 2 ripe avocados from California, freshly peeled, seeded, and sliced

Directions:

1. Toasting is optional. Begin with two slices of your preferred bread.
2. Arrange around 4 ounces of sliced turkey, a couple of lettuce leaves, and some juicy tomato slices on one piece.
3. Slices from one half of a ripe California avocado are fan-shaped on the opposite slice.
4. To taste, add salt and pepper.
5. Come together as a team and take a deep breath.

Nutrition facts:

Serving: 1g

Calories: 518kcal

Carbohydrates: 29g

Protein: 23gFat: 35g

Saturated Fat: 12g

Polyunsaturated Fat: 20g

Cholesterol: 172mg

Sodium: 1396mg

Fiber: 7gSugar: 4g

33. Italian Prosciutto Panini

Ingredients

- ¼ cup reduced-fat mayonnaise
- one 12-oz loaf of French bread, split in half horizontally
- Two tablespoons of freshly chopped basil
- One cup (four ounces) a couple of ounces of thinly sliced prosciutto
- freshly shredded mozzarella cheese
- Two plum tomatoes, cut thinly with cooking spray

Directions:

1. Remove the upper and lower halves of the bread, leaving a 1/2-inch-thick crust; save the shattered bread for a different purpose.
2. On the cut side of each bread half, spread 2 teaspoons of mayonnaise.
3. On the bottom half of the bread, scatter the 1/2 cup cheese and basil.
4. Evenly sprinkle remaining 1/2 cup cheese, tomato pieces, and prosciutto on top.
5. Fold top half of loaf over. In four equal pieces, cut the full loaf crosswise.
6. Cook for 3 minutes on each side, or until bread is toasted.
7. sandwiches cook, keep the cast-iron skillet covered.

Nutrition facts:

Per Serving: 316

calories; calories from fat 30%;

fat 10.6g;

saturated fat 4.8g;

mono fat 2.3g;

poly fat 1.9g;

protein 16.1g;

carbohydrates 39.9g;

fiber 2g;

cholesterol 31mg;

iron 2.8mg;

sodium 799mg;

calcium 196mg.

34. Korean Bibimbap Bowl

Ingredients

- ½ thinly sliced English cucumber
- A tsp of rice vinegar
- 1/4 teaspoon of toasted sesame oil
- Fresh mung bean sprouts in a cup and shredded carrots in a cup
- 4 cups of baby spinach
- 1/2 teaspoon of tamari
- 2 cups cooked white rice, short grains
- 1 cup of cubed baked tofu or two fried eggs
- Optional: 4 ounces of sautéed shiitake mushrooms
- Just one recipe Gochujang Sauce

Directions:

1. Combine the cucumber slices, ¼ teaspoon sesame oil, rice vinegar, and a dash of salt in a small bowl. Put away.
2. In a small pot, bring the water to a boil.
3. Cook the bean sprouts for one minute after adding them.
4. Empty and place aside.

Nutrition facts:

Serving: 1Serving

Calories: 327.55kcal

Carbohydrates: 20.83g

Protein: 12.58g

Fat: 11.45g

Sodium: 1003.28mg

Fiber: 3.13g

35. Poke Bowl

Ingredients

- 1 pound of premium ahi tuna;
- 2 tablespoons of soy sauce;
- 1 tablespoon of sesame oil;
- 1 tablespoon of rice vinegar;
- 1 tablespoon of honey;
- 1/4 cup of light mayo;
- 1 tablespoon of sriracha;
- 4 cups of cooked brown rice;
- 1 cup of diced cucumber;
- 1/2 cup of shredded carrots;
- 1/2 cup of shelled edamame;
- 2 large avocados, peeled and sliced;
- 1 tablespoon of black sesame seeds;
- 1 tsp green onion

Direction

1. Dice the tuna using a sharp knife.
2. Transfer the tuna, sesame oil, rice vinegar, honey, and soy sauce into a medium-sized bowl.
3. Mix by tossing.
4. While you are preparing the remaining ingredients, let the tuna sit.

5. Fill a bowl with mayo and Sriracha.

6. Mix well to blend.

7. Add little pepper and salt for seasoning.

8. Shortly into a plastic bag.

9. Trim the tip.

Nutrition facts:

Serving: 1bowl

Calories: 490kcal

Carbohydrates: 60g

Protein: 10g

Fat: 25g

Saturated Fat: 4g

Cholesterol: 2mg

Sodium: 649mg

Potassium: 754mg

Fiber: 12g

Sugar: 3g

Vitamin A: 147IU

Vitamin C: 12mg

Calcium: 63mg

Iron: 3mg

36. Lemon arugula pasta

Ingredients

- 1 pound of gemelli pasta (you may also use rigatoni, penne, etc.)
- 4 sliced cloves of garlic
- 8 ounces of baby arugula
- 2 tablespoons of fresh lemon juice or one lemon worth
- 1 tablespoon of lemon zest or one lemon worth
- 1 teaspoon of kosher salt plus additional to taste;
- 1/2 cup of grated Parmigiano Reggiano, plus enough for shaving;
- 1/2 teaspoon of crushed spicy red pepper flakes;
- 1/4 cup of extra virgin olive oil

Direction

1. Heat a big saucepan of salted water (two teaspoons kosher salt) till it boils.
2. Linguine al dente. Save the water from the pasta.
3. As the pasta cooks, preheat a large pan over medium-low heat.
4. Once the pan has warmed up for two minutes, drizzle it with extra virgin olive oil.
5. Add the red pepper flakes after one to two minutes of sautéing the garlic.
6. Continue cooking for a further 30 seconds.
7. Taste test and adjust the salt as needed.
8. Garnish with shaved Parmigiano Reggiano cheese and serve in dishes with a drizzle of extra virgin olive oil.
9. To easily shave the cheese, use a vegetable peeler. Enjoy yourself!

Nutrition facts:

Calories: 569kcal

Carbohydrates: 87.5g

Protein: 19.7g

Fat: 18.1g

Saturated Fat: 3.9g

Cholesterol: 8mg

Sodium: 659mg

Potassium: 240mg

Fiber: 5.1g

Sugar: 3.5g

Calcium: 218mg

Iron: 5mg

37. Harvest grain salad

Ingredients

- 1 cup of quinoa, prepared as directed on the package, in three cups of water
- 1/2 chopped bell pepper
- 1/4 sliced red onion, finely
- Boil and shell 1 cup of edamame (unshell 1 cup)
- approximately 8 chopped dried apricots, 1/2 cup
- I used pecans for my 1/2 cup of finely chopped nuts.
- 1/4 cup orange juice
- 2 teaspoons of red wine vinegar
- 1/2 teaspoon cumin
- 1/4 cup of blue cheese crumbles (optional)
- Add salt and pepper to taste.

Direction

1. After cooking, let the quinoa cool down.
2. Mix the quinoa with the vegetables and apricots after it has cooled.
3. Add the cumin, orange juice, red wine vinegar, salt, and pepper.
4. Mix well, and if wanted, sprinkle some blue cheese on top.
5. Serve right away or store in the refrigerator for up to a week.

38. Spicy italian chicken sausage & broccoli rabe

Ingredients

- Blade A: Two zucchini
- Salt, pepper, and 2 tablespoons of olive oil
- 2 minced cloves of garlic
- 1 tsp of chili peppers
- 2 hot Italian sausage links or a sausage made with chicken!
- 1/2 cup of chicken broth
- 1/2 bunch of broccoli rabe
- 1 tablespoon of lemon juice, optionally added sprinkle of oregano flakes
- 1/2 cup of shredded Pecorino Romano cheese

Direction

1. Arrange the broccoli rabe. After washing, pat dry the leaves.
2. Remove most of the stems, which are the thickest sections.
3. Take a peeler and remove a little bit of the stems' skin.
4. Slice till you reach the foliage. Put away
5. Put the olive oil in a big skillet and heat it to medium.
6. Add the garlic and the sausage to a skillet, slicing it into 1/2-inch chunks (you can also remove it from its casing and crumble it, depending on your preference).
7. Season with a little oregano, salt, and pepper.
8. Cook, turning occasionally, for about 3 minutes on each side.
9. Place into plates and savor!

Nutrition facts:

393	Calories
20g	Fat
36g	Carbs
19g	Protein

39. Chimichurri steak tacos

Ingredients

- 8 tortillas
- 1½ pounds of marinated flank steak
- ½ cup pepper jack cheese
- ½ cup white vinegar
- ½ cup sugar
- ½ cup apple cider vinegar
- ½ clove crushed garlic
- ½ cup your favorite chimichurri sauce
- ½ tablespoon avocado oil

Direction

1. Put the apple cider and white vinegars, sugar, garlic, and red onion in a mason jar.
2. Spoon ¾ of the chimichurri over the flank steak that has been placed in a bowl or ziploc bag. Give it a 12-hour marinade.
3. Half an hour before cooking, take the steak out of the refrigerator.
4. Heat a cast-iron pan to a medium-high temperature.
5. Brush the steak with avocado oil and sear it for about 6 minutes on each side over the cast iron. Depending on the thickness and weight of the meat, this could need to be changed.
6. I usually aim for a temperature of 125°C to 130°C for medium-rare steaks.
7. Let the steak sit for ten minutes after removing it from the grill.

Nutrition facts:

Calories: 777kcal

Carbohydrates: 36g

Protein: 45g

Fat: 48g

Saturated Fat: 12g

Polyunsaturated Fat: 5g

Monounsaturated Fat: 28g

Cholesterol: 115mg

Sodium: 620mg

Potassium: 722mg

Fiber: 3g

Sugar: 7g

Vitamin A: 109IU

Vitamin C: 2mg

Calcium: 242mg

Iron: 5mg

40. Mushroom and spinach risotto

Ingredients

- 1 liter of liquid stock reduced in Massel salt, chicken style
- 1/2 tablespoon olive oil
- Finely slice one medium brown onion.
- Sliced button mushrooms, 250g
- 1/2 cup of arborio rice
- 1/2 cup of dry white wine
- 150 grams of baby spinach
- 30g of minced butter and 3/4 cup of finely grated parmesan

Direction

1. Transfer stock to a saucepan over medium heat along with 1 cup of cold water.
2. Cook until mixture begins to boil, about 6 minutes. Turn down the heat to stay warm.
3. In a large, heavy-based saucepan, heat the oil over medium-high heat.
4. Include the mushrooms and onion.
5. Cook until onion is tender, stirring occasionally, about 5 minutes. Include rice.
6. Cook until coated, stirring, for 1 to 2 minutes.
7. Pour in the wine. Stir and cook for 30 seconds, or until the wine is absorbed.

Nutrition facts:

Kcal 574

Fat 22g

Saturates 10g

Carbs 70g

Sugars 0g

Fibre 5g

Protein 17g

Salt 1.93g

41. Sweet potato gnocchi with sage butter

Ingredients

- 2 medium-sized sweet potatoes approximately two cups mashed
- Ricotta cheese made with half a cup of whole milk.
- 1 huge egg
- 2 to 3 cups all-purpose flour
- 1 teaspoon kosher salt
- 1/4 cup of butter with salt.
- 12 little sage leaves
- Grated Parmiggiano-Reggiano cheese, half a cup
- 1/2 teaspoon of crushed red pepper flakes freshly ground
- 1/2 teaspoon of black pepper

Direction

1. Before baking, preheat the oven to 400°F.
2. Using a fork, pierce the potato all over.
3. Potatoes should be baked for 50–60 minutes, or until fork tender, on a baking sheet covered with parchment paper.
4. After cooking, cut the sweet potatoes in half, let them cool, and then puree or mash them coarsely.

Nutrition facts:

Total Fat 18.8g   34%

Cholesterol 54.2mg   18%

Sodium 890.6mg   39%

Total Carbohydrate 31.8g   12%

Dietary Fiber 3.9g 14%

Sugars 3.7g

Protein 10.2g   20%

Vitamin A 582.1μg   65%

Vitamin C 52.5mg   58%

Iron 2mg   11%

Potassium 443.9mg   9%

Phosphorus 178.1mg   14%

42. Greek chicken

Ingredients

- 1/4 cup of olive oil
- 2 squeezed lemons and three minced garlic cloves
- 1 tablespoon of freshly chopped rosemary
- 1 tsp finely chopped fresh thyme
- 1/4 tsp finely chopped fresh oregano
- 1 4-pound chicken that has been sliced

Direction

1. In a glass dish, combine olive oil, lemon juice, oregano, garlic, rosemary, and thyme.
2. Add the chicken pieces to the marinade, cover, and refrigerate for two to three hours to marinate.
3. Turn up the heat to high on an outside grill and give the grates a quick oiling.
4. After putting the chicken on the grill, discard the marinade.
5. Smaller pieces will cook more quickly.
6. Cook the chicken for about 15 minutes on each side, or until it is no longer pink at the bone and the juices flow clear.
7. Near the bone, an instant-read thermometer should register 165 degrees Fahrenheit or 74 degrees Celsius.

Nutrition facts:

412	Calories
31g	Fat
4g	Carbs
31g	Protein

43. Mexican street corn salad

Ingredients

- 4 ears of fresh corn that have been husked and extra virgin olive oil to brush
- 1/4 tsp mayo, or vegan mayo
- 1 minced clove of garlic
- 1 lime, zest and juice
- ⅓ cup of finely chopped onions
- ¼ cup of feta cheese or crumbled Cotija
- ¼ cup fresh cilantro, finely chopped
- 1/2 teaspoon of chili powder or smoked paprika
- 1 chopped jalapeño pepper* ¼ tsp sea salt

Direction

1. Heat a grill to a medium-high temperature.
2. Once the corn has developed char marks, grill it for two minutes on each side after brushing it with olive oil.
3. Take off and put aside from the grill.
4. In a big bowl, mix the lime zest, juice, garlic, and mayo.
5. Cut the corn kernels off and add them, along with the scallions, to the bowl.

Nutrition facts:

276   Calories

18g   Fat

26g   Carbs

7g   Protein

44. Spinach artichoke quesadillas

Ingredients

- 1/2 tablespoon olive oil
- ½ cup of cream cheese
- 1 tsp chopped garlic
- 8 ounces (one cup) of chopped and drained artichoke hearts
- 2 cups of baby spinach leaves
- Shredded mozzarella cheese, two cups
- 1/2 cup of shredded parmesan cheese
- 2 substantial tortillas

Direction

1. Cream cheese and olive oil should be combined in a sizable 12-inch skillet over medium heat for two to three minutes, or until the cheese has melted.
2. Add the artichokes, spinach, and minced garlic and stir.
3. Cook the spinach for two to three minutes, or until it begins to shrink.
4. Stir until melted after adding the mozzarella and parmesan cheeses.
5. Take out of the heat.
6. Cut in three triangles. Proceed with the leftover mixture and tortillas.
7. Warm or hot service is preferred.

Nutrition facts:

Calories: 368kcal

Carbohydrates: 13g

Protein: 18g

Fat: 27g

Saturated Fat: 14g

Cholesterol: 80mg

Sodium: 867mg

Potassium: 197mg

Fiber: 2g

Sugar: 3g

Vitamin A: 2215IU

Vitamin C: 4mg

Calcium: 417mg

Iron: 1mg

DINNER

45. Tofu Stir-Fry with Mixed Vegetables

Ingredients:

- 1 package Trader Joe's Extra Firm Tofu, cubed
- 2 cups mixed stir-fry vegetables (such as bell peppers, broccoli, and snap peas)
- 2 tablespoons soy sauce
- 1 tablespoon sesame oil
- 1 tablespoon honey
- Cooked rice, for serving
- 1 chopped, peeled carrot
- Chop 1 small head of bok choy,
- 2 cups fresh mushrooms, and ¼ cup bean sprouts.
- 1 cup of drained and sliced bamboo shoots
- ½ teaspoon of crushed red pepper

Directions

1. In a skillet, heat sesame oil over medium heat.

2. Add cubed tofu and cook until golden brown.

3. Add mixed vegetables to the skillet and stir-fry until tender.

4. In a small bowl, mix soy sauce and honey. Pour over the tofu and vegetables, stirring to combine.

5. Serve over cooked rice.

Nutritional Fact

Serving:	1 cup
Calories:	294 kcal
Carbohydrates:	21.5 g
Protein:	18.5 g
Fat:	16 g
Saturated Fat:	2.5 g
Sodium:	868.5 mg
Fiber:	6.5 g
Sugar:	6.5 g

46. Black Bean and Corn Quesadillas

Ingredients:

- 4 whole wheat tortillas
- 1 can Trader Joe's Cuban Style Black Beans, drained and rinsed
- 1 cup frozen corn, thawed
- ½ cup shredded Monterey Jack cheese
- 2 tablespoons chopped fresh cilantro
- Guacamole and salsa, for serving

Directions

1. Heat a skillet over medium heat. Place one tortilla in the skillet.

2. Spread black beans, corn, shredded cheese, and chopped cilantro evenly over the tortilla.

3. Top with another tortilla. Cook until the bottom tortilla is golden and crispy, then carefully flip the quesadilla

Nutritional Fact

Serving:	1quesadilla
Calories:	289.24kcal
Carbohydrates:	34.29g
Protein:	12.19g
Fat:	11.58g
Sodium:	833.43mg
Fiber:	5.29g

47. Salmon and Asparagus Foil Packets

Ingredients:

- 4 salmon fillets
- 1 bunch asparagus, trimmed
- 2 tablespoons olive oil
- 2 cloves garlic, minced
- Zest and juice of 1 lemon
- Salt and pepper to taste

Directions

1. Preheat the oven to 400°F (200°C).

2. Place each salmon fillet on a piece of aluminum foil. Arrange asparagus around the salmon.

3. In a small bowl, mix together olive oil, minced garlic, lemon zest, lemon juice, salt, and pepper.

4. Drizzle the mixture over the salmon and asparagus. Fold the foil over the salmon and asparagus to create packets.

5. Place packets on a baking sheet and bake for 12-15 minutes or until salmon is cooked through.

Nutritional Fact

Serving:	340g
Calories:	463kcal
Carbohydrates:	7g
Protein:	41g
Fat:	29g

Saturated Fat:	13g
Cholesterol:	145mg
Sodium:	404mg
Potassium:	1113mg
Fiber:	2g
Sugar:	2g
Vitamin A:	1505IU
Vitamin C:	15.4mg
Calcium:	198mg
Iron:	4mg

48. Lemon Herb Grilled Shrimp Skewers

Ingredients:

- 1 lb large shrimp, peeled and deveined
- Zest and juice of 1 lemon
- 2 cloves garlic, minced
- 2 tablespoons chopped fresh parsley
- 1 tablespoon chopped fresh dill
- 2 tablespoons olive oil
- Salt and black pepper, to taste
- Wooden skewers, soaked in water

Directions

1. In a bowl, mix lemon zest, lemon juice, minced garlic, chopped parsley, chopped dill, olive oil, salt, and black pepper.

2. Add shrimp to the bowl and toss to coat.

3. Thread shrimp onto wooden skewers.

4. Preheat the grill to medium-high heat.

5. Grill shrimp skewers for 2-3 minutes on each side or until shrimp are pink and opaque.

Nutritional Fact

Calories:	121kcal
Carbohydrates:	7g
Protein:	1g
Fat:	11g
Saturated Fat:	2g
Polyunsaturated Fat:	1g
Monounsaturated Fat:	8g
Sodium:	305mg
Potassium:	147mg
Fiber:	3g
Sugar:	2g
Vitamin A:	642IU
Vitamin C:	36mg
Calcium:	48mg
Iron:	2mg

49. Cajun Shrimp and Sausage Skillet

Ingredients:

- 1 lb large shrimp, peeled and deveined
- 12 oz Andouille sausage, sliced
- 1 red bell pepper, sliced1 green bell pepper, sliced
- 1 yellow onion, sliced
- 2 cloves garlic, minced
- 2 tablespoons Cajun seasoning
- 2 tablespoons olive oil
- Cooked rice, for serving

Directions

1. Heat olive oil in a large skillet over medium-high heat.

2. Add sliced Andouille sausage and cook until browned.

3. Add sliced bell peppers, sliced onion, and minced garlic to the skillet. Cook until vegetables are tender. Stir in Cajun seasoning.

4. Add shrimp to the skillet and cook until pink and cooked through.

5. Serve over cooked rice.

Nutritional Fact

Serving:	1 1/2 cup (1/6 of recipe)
Calories:	321kcal
Carbohydrates:	7g
Protein:	24g
Fat:	21.7g
Cholesterol:	121mg
Sodium:	101mg
Fiber:	1.7g
Sugar:	3g

50. Garlic Herb Butter Salmon

Ingredients

- 4 salmon fillets
- 4 tablespoons unsalted butter, softened
- 4 cloves garlic, minced
- 2 tablespoons chopped fresh parsley
- 1 tablespoon chopped fresh dill
- Zest of 1 lemon
- Salt and black pepper, to taste

Directions

1. Preheat the oven to 375°F (190°C).

2. In a small bowl, mix softened butter, minced garlic, chopped parsley, chopped dill, lemon zest, salt, and black pepper.

3. Place salmon fillets on a baking sheet lined with parchment paper. Spread garlic herb butter evenly over each salmon fillet.

4. Bake for 12-15 minutes or until salmon is cooked through.

Nutritional fact

Calories: 238kcal

Carbohydrates: 2g

Protein: 29g

Fat: 12g

Saturated Fat: 2g

Cholesterol: 79mg

Sodium: 397mg

Potassium: 706mg

Fiber: 1g

Sugar: 1g

Vitamin A: 108IU

Vitamin C: 2mg

Calcium: 23mg

Iron: 1mg

51. Coconut Curry Shrimp

Ingredients

- 1 lb large shrimp, peeled and deveined
- 1 can coconut milk
- 2 tablespoons red curry paste
- 1 tablespoon fish sauce
- 1 tablespoon brown sugar
- 1 red bell pepper, sliced
- 1 cup snap peas
- Cooked rice, for serving

Directions

1. In a skillet, heat coconut milk over medium heat. Stir in red curry paste, fish sauce, and brown sugar until combined.

2. Add sliced red bell pepper and snap peas to the skillet and cook until tender. Add shrimp and cook until pink and cooked through. Serve over cooked rice.

Nutritional fact

Calories 522

Fat (grams) 24 g

Sat. Fat (grams) 15 g

Carbs (grams) 31 g

Fiber (grams) 6 g

Net carbs 25

Sugar (grams) 4 g

Protein (grams) 48 g

52. Lemon Garlic Shrimp Scampi

Ingredients:

- 8 oz linguine pasta
- 1 lb large shrimp, peeled and deveined
- 4 tablespoons unsalted butter
- 4 cloves garlic, minced
- Zest and juice of 1 lemon
- ¼ cup chopped fresh parsley
- Salt and black pepper, to taste

Directions

1. Cook linguine pasta according to package instructions.

2. In a skillet, melt butter over medium heat.

3. Add minced garlic and cook until fragrant. Add shrimp and cook until pink and opaque.

4. Stir in lemon zest, lemon juice, chopped parsley, salt, and black pepper. Toss cooked pasta with the shrimp mixture.

5. Serve hot.

Nutritional fact

Calories 387kcal,

Carbohydrates 45g,

Protein 31g,

Fat 8g,

Saturated Fat 4g,

Cholesterol 300mg,

Sodium 2689mg,

Potassium 290mg,

Fiber 2g, Sugar 2g,

Vitamin A 345IU,

Vitamin C 21.6mg,

Calcium 186mg,

Iron 3.5mg

53. Mediterranean Quinoa Salad

Ingredients:

- 1 cup cooked Trader Joe's Organic Quinoa
- 1/2 cup diced cucumber
- 1/2 cup halved cherry tomatoes
- 1/4 cup sliced Kalamata olives
- 1/4 cup crumbled feta cheese
- 2 tablespoons chopped fresh parsley
- 2 tablespoons lemon juice
- 1 tablespoon olive oil
- Salt and black pepper, to taste

Directions:

1. In a large bowl, combine cooked quinoa, diced cucumber, cherry tomatoes, Kalamata olives, crumbled feta cheese, chopped parsley, lemon juice, and olive oil.
2. Season with salt and black pepper.
3. Toss to combine.
4. Serve chilled or at room temperature.

NUTRITION FACT

5. Calories: 262kcal
6. Carbohydrates: 19g
7. Protein: 13g
8. Fat: 16g
9. Saturated Fat: 3g
10. Polyunsaturated Fat: 5g
11. Monounsaturated Fat: 6g
12. Trans Fat: 0.02g
13. Cholesterol: 83mg
14. Sodium: 691mg
15. Potassium: 396mg
16. Fiber: 5g
17. Sugar: 3g
18. Vitamin A: 624IU
19. Vitamin C: 19mg
20. Calcium: 136mg
21. Iron: 1mg

54. Spicy Korean beef bowl

Ingredients:

- 1/2 cup packed brown sugar and 1/2 cup soy sauce with less sodium
- Sesame oil, two tsp
- 1/2 tsp finely crushed red pepper flakes, or additional to taste
- 1/2 teaspoon of ground ginger
- A single spoonful of vegetable oil
- minced three garlic cloves
- A single pound of ground beef
- ¼ teaspoon sesame seeds; two finely sliced green onions

Directions

1. Combine the ginger, brown sugar, soy sauce, sesame oil, and red pepper flakes in a small bowl.
2. In a large cast iron skillet set over medium-high heat, heat the vegetable oil.
3. Add the garlic and simmer, stirring frequently, for about one minute, or until fragrant.
4. Add the ground beef and heat for 3 to 5 minutes, or until browned, crumbling the meat occasionally; drain any excess grease

55. Creamy mushroom and spinach pasta

Ingredients:

- 2 tablespoons of olive oil
- 1 small onion, diced finely
- 1/2 150g tagliatelle and 150g baby mushrooms
- 200g of low-fat crème fraîche and two smashed garlic cloves
- 15g grated Parmesan cheese, or vegetarian cheese of choice
- 120 grams of baby spinach
- ½ teaspoon of optional chili flakes

Directions

1. In a medium saucepan, heat the oil over medium heat.
2. Fry the onion and mushrooms for 10 minutes, or until they are softened and gently browned. Meanwhile, prepare the pasta as directed on the package.
3. Cook for a further two minutes after adding the garlic to the pan with the mushrooms.
4. After adding the young spinach, stir to mix in the crème fraîche and parmesan cheese.
5. Put away.

Nutritional fact

Kcal 491

Fa t20g

Saturates 6g

Carbs 49g

Sugars 7g

Fibre 5g

Protein 27g

Salt 1g

56. Garlic shrimp Alfredo

Ingredients:

- Peeled, deveined, and tailless shrimp, weighing one pound, any size
- To make shrimp garlic powder, use one to two tablespoons of butter, depending on desire.
- 1 and 1/2 cups butter
- 16 ounces of heavy cream, two chopped cloves of garlic
- A quarter-teaspoon of white pepper
- 1/2 cup of grated Parmesan cheese
- 34 oz. of mozzarella cheese

Directions

1. Add one or two tablespoons of melted butter to a pan.
2. Garlic powder should be applied liberally to the shrimp.
3. Once cooked, stir from time to time. Remove from the way.
4. Lightly brown butter in a small saucepan.
5. When the garlic is tender, approximately two minutes, add it and cook it.
6. Simmer for 8 to 10 minutes after adding the heavy cream and pepper. Include.
7. Stir in the Parmesan cheese and simmer for an additional 5 to 8 minutes.

Nutritional fact

Calories **541**

Total Fat **26g**

Saturated Fat 16g

Trans Fat 1g

Unsaturated Fat 10g

Cholesterol **135mg**

Sodium **325mg**

Carbohydrates **54g**

Fiber 2g

Sugar 7g

Protein **23g**

57. Vegan pesto zoodles

Ingredients:

- 6 medium zucchini (a total of two and a half pounds), trimmed
- 1/4 tsp salt, separated
- 1 cup of tightly packed, fresh basil leaves
- 2 peeled and smashed garlic cloves
- ⅓ cup cashews, unsalted
- 2 to 3 tablespoons of lemon juice
- 2 tsp of nutritional yeast
- 1/2 teaspoon of ground pepper
- 1/4 cup of extra virgin olive oil plus 1 tablespoon, divided
- 1/2 cup of grape tomatoes

Directions

1. With a vegetable peeler or spiral slicer, thinly slice the zucchini lengthwise into long, thin strands or strips.
2. If slicing vegetables using a vegetable slicer, stop when you come to the central seeds (they cause the noodles to crumble).
3. Toss the zucchini "noodles" with 1/4 teaspoon salt after placing them in a colander.
4. After letting it drain for ten to fifteen minutes, gently press out any remaining water.

Nutritional fact

Serving: 1cup (1/4 recipe)

Calories: 442kcal

Carbohydrates: 26.7g

Protein: 17.4g

Fat: 34.9g

Saturated Fat: 3.6g

Sodium: 340mg

Potassium: 1626mg

Fiber: 11.6g

Sugar: 7.6g

Calcium: 90mg

Iron: 8.8mg

58. Black bean and sweet potato tacos

Ingredients:

- 1 ½ pounds sweet potatoes (approximately 6 cups), cut into ½" cubes;
- 4 Tablespoons olive oil (divided);
- 1 teaspoon each of ground cumin, paprika, garlic powder, onion powder, and ground coriander;
- 1 teaspoon sea salt;
- 1 ½ cups green pepper (2 medium peppers), cut into 1" pieces;
- 1 cup red pepper (1 medium pepper), cut into 1" pieces;
- 14.5 ounces black beans (drained and rinsed);
- 1 ½ cup frozen yellow corn (thawed and drained);

Directions

1. Preheat the oven to 425 degrees Fahrenheit.
2. Grease a large baking sheet generously; mix together the spices in a small bowl and set it aside.
3. Drizzle the honey-lime cilantro sauce over all the vegetables in the pan, stirring to coat everything evenly.
4. Transfer the pan back to the oven and bake for 10 to 15 minutes, stirring occasionally, or until the corn is starting to brown and the sauce has adhered to the vegetables.
5. Take the pan out of the oven and serve right away, either in tortillas or over salad greens, garnished with your preferred taco toppings (guacamole, salsa, etc.).

Nutritional fact

Serving: 1cup

Calories: 325.8kcal

Carbohydrates: 42.2g

Protein: 15.8g

Fat: 11.6g

Saturated Fat: 2.4g

Polyunsaturated Fat: 1.3g

Monounsaturated Fat: 5.1g

Cholesterol: 40mg

Sodium: 57.4mg

Potassium: 399.2mg

Fiber: 6.3g

Sugar: 12.4g

Vitamin A: 21150IU

Vitamin C: 98.2mg

Calcium: 34mg

Iron: 2.3mg

59. Fish tacos with mango salsa

Ingredients:

- 2 fully ripe, fresh mangoes sliced and skinned;
- 1/2 cup finely chopped red onion;
- 1-2 jalapeños, seeds and membrane removed, chopped finely;
- 1/3 cup chopped cilantro stems and leaves; 2 limes, juiced; and
- 1/2 teaspoon Morton kosher salt
- 1 1/2 Tablespoons avocado or vegetable oil;
- 1 Tablespoon honey;
- 1 1/2 teaspoons chili powder;
- 1 1/2 teaspoons cumin;
- 1.5 pounds of cod, divided into 1.5-inch pieces; and

Directions

1. Turn the oven on to 450 degrees. Mango, onion, jalapeño, cilantro, lime juice, and salt should all be combined in a medium-sized bowl. Put away.
2. Combine the cod, oil, honey, paprika, cumin, chili powder, onion powder, garlic, cayenne, and salt in a big bowl.
3. Put parchment paper on a sizable baking sheet.
4. Put parchment paper on a sizable baking sheet. Place the fish pieces about 1 inch apart on the sheet after transferring it.

5. For eight to ten minutes, bake. Watch constantly to prevent burning and broil for 3 to 5 minutes, or until lightly browned. Put tacos together.

Nutritional fact

Calories: 411kcal |

Carbohydrates: 51g |

Protein: 35g |

Fat: 9g |

Saturated Fat: 1g |

Polyunsaturated Fat: 2g |

Monounsaturated Fat: 5g |

Cholesterol: 73mg |

Sodium: 1006mg |

Fiber: 7g |

Sugar: 21g

60. Falafel and hummus wraps

Ingredients:

- 4 tsp hummus (store-bought or homemade)
- 2 flatbreads made entirely of wheat
- For cooking falafel, use three tablespoons of extra virgin olive oil.
- 2 tspn of chili sauce (we use Sriracha for Harissa) is optional.
- 4r tablespoons of fresh parsley, freshly chopped
- 2 chopped tomatoes; ½ cup peeled, seeded, and diced cucumber
- Finely chopped half of a red onion
- 1 tsp extra virgin olive oil
- 1 tsp lemon juice
- 1/2 teaspoon each of salt and freshly ground black pepper

Directions

1. HEAT a big skillet over medium heat with three tablespoons of olive oil.
2. Using the palm of your hand, gently flatten golf ball-sized spoonfuls of the falafel mixture (approximately 1 heaping tablespoon for 8–10 patties); moisten your hands beforehand to help prevent sticking.
3. ACCORDINGLY PLNCH the chopped salad on top.
4. PERSONALLY TOPEACH with 4–5 falafel patties, and if desired, cover with chili sauce. Seal-side down, place the flatbreads on a baking pan that has been warmed and broil for about 15 minutes, or until crisp.

5. ROLL up the flatbreads firmly.

6. HANDLE each in half for serving.

Nutritional fact

Calories: 376

Total Fat: 14g

Saturated Fat: 2g

Trans Fat: 0g

Unsaturated Fat: 11g

Cholesterol: 0mg

Sodium: 336mg

Carbohydrates: 53g

Fiber: 10g

Sugar: 6g

Protein: 12g

61. Korean BBQ beef tacos

Ingredients:

- 1 pound of top sirloin or flank steak, cut into thin, short strips like in a stir-fry
- I enjoy the Bibigo brand of Korean BBQ sauce, which is 1/2 cup.
- Mix 1/2 red onion (thinly chopped into strips) with rice wine vinegar.
- 2 cups of prepared chopped salad or slaw mix (see notes) in a bag
- 1 green onion, thinly sliced in both the green and white parts
- 2 tablespoons of freshly chopped cilantro
- 10 to 12 little wheat tortillas for street tacos
- 2 limes, cut into little wedges

Directions

1. In a sizable mixing bowl, combine the steak strips and Korean BBQ sauce.
2. For at least two hours (or overnight), cover and let the food marinade in the refrigerator.
3. To make the tacos, put the red onion strips in a shallow serving bowl and pour half vinegar and half water over them.
4. Allow the onions to soak as you work to create a rapid pickling that will soften the more assertive flavors.
5. Let visitors construct their own tacos by serving the steak, salad mix, onions, lime quarters, and reserved cilantro separately. (To add more zest to a taco, squeeze a lime wedge over it.)

62. Turkey and avocado BLT wrap

Ingredients:

- 1 medium avocado
- 2 tsp sour cream or mayonnaise
- 1 tablespoon of brand-new lime juice
- Pepper and salt
- 1 10-to 12-inch tortillas or wraps
- 8 oz of deli turkey with shavings
- 1 cups fresh spinach, chopped or torn
- 1 cup of broccoli slaw mix or shredded carrots
- 1 English cucumber, sliced thinly like matchsticks
- 1 cup of grape or cherry tomatoes, cut in half
- Thinly slice two bell peppers (orange, red, yellow, or green).
- ½ cup Parmesan cheese, finely shredded (optional)
- Vinegar and oil (optional).
- Pepper and salt

Directions

1. Apply a few teaspoons of the avocado spread to each wrap before assembling (leaving a small border around the edge).
2. Arrange the following ingredients in layers on one half of the wrap: cucumbers, cherry tomatoes, bell peppers, turkey, spinach, carrots (or broccoli slaw), and Parmesan cheese.

3. Chop in half.

4. The avocado spread can be served right away or chilled for about an hour, well covered.

5. The avocado spread won't lose flavor if it is refrigerated for longer than that.

Nutritional fact

Serving: 1 wrap,

Calories: 407kcal,

Carbohydrates: 53g,

Protein: 22g,

Fat: 13g,

Saturated Fat: 5g,

Cholesterol: 29mg,

Sodium: 1377mg,

Fiber: 8g,

Sugar: 9g

63. Sweet and sour chicken stir-fry

Ingredients:

- 2 tsp of vegetable oil
- Cubed one-pound skinless, boneless chicken breast meat
- Cup of carrot slices,
- 1 Sliced green bell pepper, ½ cup
- Slicing ½ cup of red bell pepper
- 1 minced garlic clove
- 1/4 cup soy sauce reduced in sodium
- 1 tablespoon cornflour
- 1 8-oz can of chunky pineapple with retained juice
- 1 tablespoon vinegar
- 1 spoonful of brown sugar
- 1/4 tsp ground ginger

Directions

1. In a big skillet over medium-high heat, heat the oil.
2. Add chicken to hot oil and cook, stirring, until browned.
3. For one to two minutes, stir-fry the carrot, bell peppers, and garlic.
4. In a small dish, whisk together the cornstarch and soy sauce until thoroughly blended, then transfer to the skillet.

5. Add pineapple juice, vinegar, brown sugar, and ginger, and stir.

6. Once the sauce thickens, bring to a rolling boil.

Nutritional fact

259	Calories
9g	Fat
20g	Carbs
24g	Protein

64. Spicy tofu and veggie stir-fry

Ingredients:

- ½ tablespoons chili crunch sauce;
- 5 tablespoons low-sodium soy sauce;
- 1 tablespoon light brown sugar;
- 2 tablespoons of cornstarch or arrowroot powder; one package of extra firm tofu that has been drained, pressed, and cut into cubes
- ½ teaspoon grated ginger;
- 1 jar of diced roasted red peppers;
- 1 small bunch of broccolini, roughly chopped;
- 2 minced garlic cloves;

Directions

1. Combine the lava sauce ingredients in a small bowl and set it aside.
2. After removing the tofu block from its packaging liquid, place two paper towels on a platter and top with the entire block.
3. After placing two more paper towels on top of the tofu, place a heavy object on top of that.
4. It's heavy enough to press out moisture, but not so heavy as to crush the tofu entirely.
5. Take out of the skillet, place the tofu on a plate, and reserve.

6. Garlic, ginger, broccolini, and red peppers should all be added to the same skillet over medium heat.

7. Simmer the broccolini for 5 to 7 minutes, or until it has softened.

8. Re-add the tofu after adding the sauce and bringing it to a gentle heat.

9. After coating everything, remove from the heat and stir.

Nutritional fact

Serving: 1serving,

Calories: 207kcal,

Carbohydrates: 25g,

Protein: 17g,

Fat: 4g,

Saturated Fat: 1g,

Sodium: 2341mg,

Potassium: 426mg,

Fiber: 1g,

Sugar: 11g

65. Tortilla soup with chicken

Ingredients:

- 1 tablespoon olive oil
- 1 chopped onion;
- 3 minced large cloves of garlic;
- 1 diced and seeded jalapeño;
- 3 cups chicken broth;
- 14 and 1/2 ounces of crushed tomatoes;
- 14 and1/2 ounces of can black beans;
- 10 ounces of canned diced tomatoes with chiles, like Rotel;
- 2 boneless, skinless chicken breasts;
- 1 cup of drained canned corn;
- 1-slice cup of cilantro;
- 1 lime juiced; and finally,
- 1 sliced avocado for garnish.

Directions

1. The tortillas should be cut into ¼-inch strips for the tortilla strips.
2. One-quarter cup vegetable oil should be heated on medium-high heat in a small pan.
3. In small batches, add the tortillas to the oil and cook them for approximately a minute on each side, or until they are crisp.

4. With two forks, shred the chicken after removing it from the pot.

5. Return the shredded chicken to the pot and boil it for a further three minutes.

6. Use pepper and salt to taste and season.

7. Spoon soup into bowls; garnish with avocado slices, tortilla strips, and lime wedges.

Nutritional fact

Serving: 1.25cup

Calories: 278

Carbohydrates: 27g

Protein: 18g

Fat: 11g

Saturated Fat: 1g

Cholesterol: 36mg

Sodium: 671mg

Potassium: 714mg

Fiber: 6g

Sugar: 4g

Vitamin A: 290IU

Vitamin C: 19.9mg

Calcium: 69mg

Iron: 2.7mg

66. Ginger beef stir-fry

Ingredients:

- 1/2 cup of vegetable broth
- ⅓ cup soy sauce reduced in sodium
- 2 tsp honey powder (like Savory Spice®)
- 2 teaspoons of freshly chopped ginger
- 1 tsp of sesame oil
- 1 tablespoon cornflour
- minced three garlic cloves
- A single pinch of red pepper flakes
- A single spoonful of vegetable oil
- 1-pound skirt steak, sliced thinly across the diagonal
- 11/2 teaspoon of salt
- 2 14.5-oz packets of frozen stir-fried veggies

Directions

1. In a small bowl, combine vegetable broth, soy sauce, red pepper flakes, ginger, sesame oil, cornstarch, and garlic.
2. Vegetable oil should be boiling hot in a wok. Stir in the skirt steak, pepper, and salt.
3. For about five minutes, cook until browned.
4. Add the stir-fried veggies.

5. Add sauce mixture. Simmer the vegetables for 5 minutes or until they are thoroughly heated.

Nutritional fact

189	Calories
12g	Fat
12g	Carbs
15g	Protein

67. Italian sausage and kale soup

Ingredients:

- A single spoonful of olive oil
- Remove the casings from 1 pound of Italian sausage and replace with chicken or turkey Italian sausage, if preferred.
- 1 medium onion, two chopped carrots, and two chopped celery stalks
- 3 finely chopped garlic cloves
- Diced tomatoes, 15 ounces, cooked over fire
- 6 glasses Noose! Well,
- 1 bay leaf
- 1 dried sprig of thyme or one teaspoon
- 1 dried or one rosemary sprig
- Rinsed and drained 15 ounces of cannellini beans
- 1 bunch of lacinato kale with the rough stems cut off
- 2 tsp freshly squeezed lemon juice

Directions

1. In a large soup pot or Dutch oven over medium heat, heat the oil.

2. After adding the Italian sausage, heat it for around 8 minutes, breaking it up with a wooden spoon, until it becomes browned and fully cooked.

Nutritional fact

Calories: **406kcal,**

Carbohydrates: **25g,**

Protein: **19g,**

Fat: **27g,**

Saturated Fat: **9g,**

Polyunsaturated Fat: **4g,**

Monounsaturated Fat: **13g,**

Cholesterol: **57mg,**

Sodium: **1720mg,**

Potassium: **751mg,**

Fiber: **5g,**

Sugar: **4g,**

Vitamin A: **8863IU,**

Vitamin C: **79mg,**

Calcium: **181mg,**

Iron: **4mg**

APPETIZERS

68. Mediterranean Chickpea and Couscous Salad

Ingredients:

- 1 cup cooked Trader Joe's Harvest Grains Blend (couscous, orzo, garbanzo beans, and red quinoa)
- 1 can Trader Joe's Organic Garbanzo Beans, drained and rinsed
- 1 cup diced cucumber
- 1 cup halved cherry tomatoes
- 1/4 cup diced red onion
- 1/4 cup chopped fresh parsley
- 2 tablespoons lemon juice
- 2 tablespoons olive oil
- Salt and black pepper, to taste

Directions:

1. In a large bowl, combine cooked harvest grains blend, garbanzo beans, diced cucumber, cherry tomatoes, diced red onion, and chopped parsley.

2. Drizzle with lemon juice and olive oil. Season with salt and black pepper.

3. Toss gently to combine. Serve chilled.

69. Strawberry Greek Yogurt Popsicles

Ingredients:

- 1 cup Trader Joe's Greek Yogurt
- 1 cup sliced strawberries
- 2 tablespoons honey or maple syrup
- 2 tablespoons freshly squeezed lemon juice
- 1 teaspoon vanilla

Directions:

1. In a blender, combine Greek yogurt, sliced strawberries, and honey or maple syrup.

2. Blend until smooth. Pour the mixture into popsicle molds. Insert popsicle sticks and freeze for at least 4 hours or until solid.

3. Run warm water over the molds to release the popsicles before serving.

Nutrition fact

Calories: 104kcal

Carbohydrates: 18g

Protein: 6g

Fat: 1g

Saturated Fat: 1g

Polyunsaturated Fat: 1g

Monounsaturated Fat: 1g

Cholesterol: 3mg

Sodium: 24mg

Potassium: 87mg

Fiber: 1g

Sugar: 16g

Vitamin A: 39IU

Vitamin C: 30mg

Calcium: 75mg

Iron: 1mg

70. Frozen Banana Dipped in Chocolate

Ingredients:

- 2 ripe bananas, peeled and cut in half
- 1/2 cup chocolate chips
- 1 tablespoon coconut oil
- Toppings of choice (such as chopped nuts, shredded coconut, or sprinkles)

Directions:

1. After peeling, cut the bananas into thirds. (I think this is the perfect size, but you can also cut them into quarters or in half for smaller pops.) Make sure a plate or baking sheet will fit on a level shelf in your freezer before lining it with parchment paper. After placing the popsicle sticks about two thirds of the way into the bananas' centers, place the bananas on the lined pan. Put the pan in the freezer for four hours or overnight, or until the bananas are frozen solid.

2. Melt the chocolate after the bananas have frozen. An inch of water should be added to a small saucepan and heated to a boil over medium-high heat. Put the chocolate chips and coconut oil in a dish that fits tightly over the top of the pan and is safe to be heated. After placing the bowl over the water-filled pan, allow the chocolate chips to be softly melted by the steam. Blend until a smooth consistency is achieved.

3. Carefully lift each frozen banana over the bowl of melted chocolate one at a time, then use a spoon to evenly drizzle the chocolate over the banana's whole surface. Allow any unused chocolate to return to the dish.

4. Make sure the toppings, such as chopped peanuts, are available and close by if you want to add them. It's best to have an empty plate close to the melted chocolate bowl so you can quickly flip the banana over and add any desired toppings. As you hover the banana over the plate, any drips will be collected by it. Work fast, as the chocolate can set in as little as 60 to 90 seconds.

5. Continue with the remaining bananas, and as soon as the chocolate has solidified, put them back in the pan prepared with parchment. Until the time comes to serve them, store the pan in the freezer. Bananas that have been frozen for up to three months can be kept in the freezer in an airtight container.

Nutritional fact

Calories: 130kcal

Carbohydrates: 19g

Protein: 1g

Saturated Fat: 4g

Cholesterol: 2mg

Sodium: 11mg

Potassium: 141mg

Fiber: 1g

Sugar: 14g

Vitamin A: 59IU

Vitamin C: 4mg

Calcium: 19mg

Iron: 0.3mg

71. No-Bake Almond Butter Bars

Ingredients:

- 1 cup Trader Joe's Rolled Oats
- 1/2 cup almond butter
- 1/4 cup honey or maple syrup
- 1/4 cup chopped almonds
- 1/4 cup mini chocolate chips
- Pinch of salt

Directions

1. Combine 1 cup almond butter, almond flour, agave nectar, 2 tablespoons coconut oil, and salt in a medium-sized bowl to make the almond butter layer.

2. Spread the almond butter mixture evenly across a parchment paper-lined bread pan.

3. Heat the chocolate chips in a small bowl in the microwave, stirring every 30 seconds, until the chips are smooth.

4. Mix the two tablespoons of almond butter and one tablespoon of coconut oil for the chocolate layer into the melted chocolate by whisking them in.

5. After spreading the chocolate over the layer of almond butter, freeze for one hour.

6. To take the bars out of the pan, run a knife along the pan's edges and lift the parchment paper up.

7. Slice into twelve bars.

Nutritional fact

- Serving Size: 1 bar
- Calories: 374
- Sugar: 12g
- Sodium: 57mg
- Fat: 30.7g
- Saturated Fat: 7.1g
- Unsaturated Fat: 0g
- Trans Fat: 0g
- Carbohydrates: 20.5g
- Fiber: 6.5g
- Protein: 8.5g
- Cholesterol: 2mg

72. Berry Chia Seed Pudding

Ingredients:

- 1/4 cup Trader Joe's Chia Seeds
- 1 cup almond milk
- 1 tablespoon honey or maple syrup
- 1/2 teaspoon vanilla extract
- Mixed berries for topping

Directions:

1. In a jar or bowl, mix chia seeds, almond milk, honey or maple syrup, and vanilla extract.

2. Stir well and refrigerate for at least 2 hours or overnight.

3. Top with mixed berries before serving.

Nutritional fact

Calories 343

Fat   15g

Carbs   39g

Protein 14g

73. Chocolate Covered Strawberries

Ingredients:

- 1 cup chocolate chips
- 1 tablespoon coconut oil
- 10-12 strawberries

Directions

1. First, give the strawberries a good wash, and then make sure they dry completely. As you may know, chocolate and water don't mix well, which is why it's crucial to thoroughly dry the strawberries! The chocolate won't adhere if the strawberries are even slightly moist!

2. Place a few toppings, such as coconut or broken nuts, onto each individual tiny plate if desired. Use parchment or waxed paper to line a sheet pan.

3. Melt the chocolate in the microwave or over a double boiler (follow the directions in the post above), taking out and stirring the chocolate after 30 seconds. Don't let the chocolate burn by stirring it frequently!

4. While still holding the stem of the strawberry, dip it into the melted chocolate, lift it, and twist it slightly so that the extra chocolate falls back into the bowl. The strawberry can now be placed on the parchment paper after being dipped in coconut or almonds, or left unadorned. With the remaining strawberries, repeat.

5. Dip a fork into the melted white chocolate and pour it over the strawberries to create a white chocolate drenched strawberry.

6. Chill the strawberries for 15 minutes or until the chocolate solidifies.

Nutritional fact

Calories	115
Fat	7g
Carbs	13g
Protein	1g

74. Stuffed Mini Peppers

Ingredients:

- 12 mini sweet peppers
- 4 oz Trader Joe's Goat Cheese
- 2 tablespoons chopped fresh herbs (such as basil, parsley, or chives)
- Salt and pepper to taste
- 2 tbsp extra virgin olive oil salt
- 10 ounce log goat cheese softened (soft chèvre)
- 2/3 cup grated parmesan (40g by weight)
- 1 tbsp minced garlic
- 2 jalapeños seeded and finely chopped (1/3 cup, measured)
- 1/4 tsp freshly ground black pepper

Directions:

1. Preheat the oven to 375°F (190°C).

2. Cut the tops off the mini peppers and remove the seeds. In a bowl, mix together goat cheese, chopped fresh herbs, salt, and pepper.

3. `Stuff each mini pepper with the goat cheese mixture.

4. Place the stuffed peppers on a baking sheet lined with parchment paper.

5. Bake for 10-12 minutes or until the peppers are tender and the cheese is slightly melted.

Nutritional fact

calories: 28kcal

protein: 1g

fat: 2g

saturated fat: 1g

cholesterol: 3mg

sodium: 41mg

potassium: 23mg

vitamin a: 360IU

vitamin c: 12.2mg

calcium: 23mg

iron: 0.2mg

75. Spinach and Artichoke Dip

Ingredients:

- 1 package Trader Joe's Frozen Chopped Spinach, thawed and drained
- 1 can Trader Joe's Artichoke Hearts, drained and chopped
- 1 cup Trader Joe's Shredded Mozzarella Cheese
- 1/2 cup Trader Joe's Grated Parmesan Cheese
- 1/2 cup Trader Joe's Greek Yogurt
- 1/4 cup mayonnaise
- 2 cloves garlic, minced
- Salt and pepper to taste
- Trader Joe's Pita Chips for serving

Directions:

1. Preheat the oven to 375°F (190°C).

2. In a bowl, mix together chopped spinach, chopped artichoke hearts, shredded mozzarella cheese, grated parmesan cheese, Greek yogurt, mayonnaise, minced garlic, salt, and pepper.

3. Transfer the mixture to a baking dish.

4. Bake for 25-30 minutes or until bubbly and golden brown.

5. Serve hot with Trader Joe's Pita Chips

Nutritional fact

Calories from Fat	180%
Daily Value*	
Fat 20g	31%
Saturated Fat 9g	56%
Cholesterol 49mg	16%
Sodium 440mg	19%
Potassium 259mg	7%
Carbohydrates 6g	2%
Fiber 2g	8%
Sugar 1g	1%
Protein 8g	16%
Vitamin A 3115IU	62%
Vitamin C 3.9mg	5%
Calcium 220mg	22%
Iron 0.9mg	5%

76. Spinach and Feta Stuffed Chicken Breast

Ingredients:

- 4 boneless, skinless chicken breasts
- 1 cup cooked spinach, squeezed dry
- 1/2 cup crumbled feta cheese
- 2 cloves garlic, minced
- Salt and black pepper, to taste
- Olive oil, for drizzling

Directions:

1. Preheat the oven to 350 degrees.
2. Prepare chicken for stuffing.(You can either slice 2 thick chicken breasts in half and make 4, or beat 4 chicken breasts until thin and wide.).
3. Cook spinach in garlic and oil on top of the stove until done.
4. Add in feta cheese and mix well. (You can add as much as you like. I LOVE feta cheese!).
5. Distribute spinach mixture onto each chicken breast. (You may have some leftovers).
6. Wrap chicken around the mixture (kinda like a taco) and secure with a toothpick.
7. Roll each breast in breadcrumbs until well coated.
8. Place in a glass baking dish and pour butter over them.
9. Cook for 30 minutes and serve.

Nutritional Fact

- Calories: 401kcal
- Carbohydrates: 39g
- Protein: 32g
- Fat: 32g
- Saturated Fat: 15g
- Cholesterol: 94mg
- Sodium: 560mg
- Potassium: 970mg

Made in the USA
Las Vegas, NV
07 December 2024

13513957R10083